EARLY PEOPLES

ANCIENT GREEKS

WORLD
BOOK

World Book
a Scott Fetzer company
Chicago
www.worldbookonline.com

World Book, Inc.
233 N. Michigan Avenue
Chicago, IL 60601
U.S.A.

For information about other World Book publications, visit our Web site at http://www.worldbookonline.com or call 1-800-WORLDBK (967-5325). For information about sales to schools and libraries, call 1-800-975-3250 (United States), or 1-800-837-5365 (Canada).

Library of Congress Cataloging-in-Publication Data

Ancient Greeks.
    p. cm. – (Early peoples)
    Includes index.
    Summary: "A discussion of the early Greeks, including who the people were, where they lived, the rise of civilization, social structure, religion, art and architecture, science and technology, daily life, entertainment and sports. Features include timelines, fact boxes, glossary, list of recommended reading and Web sites, and index"–Provided by publisher.
    ISBN 978-0-7166-2130-0
    1. Greece–Civilization–To 146 B.C.–Juvenile literature.
I. World Book, Inc.
DF77.A596 2009
938--dc22

                                    2008035512

Printed in China
1 2 3 4 5 13 12 11 10 09

STAFF

EXECUTIVE COMMITTEE
President
 Paul A. Gazzolo
Vice President and Chief Marketing Officer
 Patricia Ginnis
Vice President and Chief Financial Officer
 Donald D. Keller
Vice President and Editor in Chief
 Paul A. Kobasa
Director, Human Resources
 Bev Ecker
Chief Technology Officer
 Tim Hardy
Managing Director, International
 Benjamin Hinton

EDITORIAL
Editor in Chief
 Paul A. Kobasa
Associate Director, Supplementary Publications
 Scott Thomas
Managing Editor, Supplementary Publications
 Barbara A. Mayes
Senior Editor, Supplementary Publications
 Kristina Vaicikonis
Manager, Research, Supplementary Publications
 Cheryl Graham
Manager, Contracts & Compliance
(Rights & Permissions)
 Loranne K. Shields
Administrative Assistant
 Ethel Matthews

Editors
 Nicholas Kilzer
 Scott Richardson
 Christine Sullivan

GRAPHICS AND DESIGN
Associate Director
 Sandra M. Dyrlund
Manager
 Tom Evans
Coordinator, Design Development and Production
 Brenda B. Tropinski

EDITORIAL ADMINISTRATION
Director, Systems and Projects
 Tony Tills
Senior Manager, Publishing Operations
 Timothy Falk

PRODUCTION
Director, Manufacturing and Pre-Press
 Carma Fazio
Manufacturing Manager
 Steve Hueppchen
Production/Technology Manager
 Anne Fritzinger
Production Specialist
 Curley Hunter
Proofreader
 Emilie Schrage

MARKETING
Chief Marketing Officer
 Patricia Ginnis
Associate Director, School and Library Marketing
 Jennifer Parello

Produced for World Book by
 White-Thomson Publishing Ltd.
+44 (0)845 362 8240
www.wtpub.co.uk
Steve White-Thomson, President

Writer: Michael Burgan
Editor: Robert Famighetti
Designer: Clare Nicholas
Photo Researcher: Amy Sparks
Map Artist: Stefan Chabluk
Illustrators: Adam Hook (p. 18),
 Stefan Chabluk (pp. 36-37)
Fact Checker: Charlene Rimsa
Proofreader: Catherine Gardner
Indexer: Nila Glikin

Consultant:
Philip de Souza
Lecturer in Classics and
Vice-Head, School of Classics
University College Dublin, Ireland

TABLE OF CONTENTS

Glossary There is a glossary on pages 60-61. Terms defined in the glossary are in type **that looks like this** on their first appearance on any spread (two facing pages).

Additional Resources Books for further reading and recommended Web sites are listed on page 62. Because of the nature of the Internet, some Web site addresses may have changed since publication. The publisher has no responsibility for any such changes or for the content of cited sources.

WHO WERE THE ANCIENT GREEKS?

▲ The ancient Greek world was centered around the Aegean Sea. The Greeks spread their culture to Ionia, in what is now Turkey, and even farther beyond their original homelands.

Massive buildings, great works of art, words that make people laugh or cry—the ancient Greeks left behind all these achievements and more. Although they lived more than 2,000 years ago, the Greeks' role in world history is still felt today.

The ancient Greeks were based in what is now the nation of Greece. They also lived in southern Italy, western Turkey, and other areas along the Mediterranean (*medh uh tuh RAY nee uhn*), Aegean (*ih JEE uhn*), and Black Seas. For hundreds of years, most Greeks lived in **city-states** consisting of a main city surrounded by smaller villages and farms. The Greek city-states were independent—each ran its own affairs. The residents of the different cities shared a similar language, **culture,** and religion. Sometimes the city-states battled each other; at other times they united to face a common enemy.

The Importance of Athens

The major city-states included Athens (*ATH ihnz* or *ATH uhnz*), Corinth (*KAWR ihnth*), Sparta (*SPAHR tuh*), and Thebes (*theebz*). They were located on two **peninsulas** (*puh NIHN suh luhz*) in southern Greece—Attica and the Peloponnesus (*PEHL uh puh NEE suhs*).

Athens was one of the most advanced of the Greek city-states. It reached its peak in the 400's B.C., as the city gained great wealth and influence that extended across the Aegean Sea into what is now Turkey. Athens produced many of ancient Greece's greatest artists, writers, and thinkers. Many of the ideas born in Athens thousands of years ago are still taught today.

The Spread of Greek Ideas

In 334 B.C., a Greek king and general named Alexander the Great began to conquer foreign lands. His **empire** helped spread Greek culture across Africa and Asia. The Greeks called themselves Hellenes *(HEHL eenz)*, and their culture is sometimes called Hellenic *(heh LEHN ihk)* or Hellenistic *(HEHL uh NIHS tihk)*. The influence of Greek culture continued after Alexander's empire collapsed, and the Greek language influenced many others. For example, many English words have their roots in ancient Greek words. Education, art, and government as we know them today trace their roots to the Greeks and the people they influenced.

▲ Athens' major landmark is a hill known as the Acropolis *(uh KROP uh lihs)*. On the Acropolis, the ancient Greeks built **temples** in honor of their gods. The largest and most impressive is the Parthenon *(PAHR thuh non)*, a temple to the goddess Athena.

TIMELINE OF ANCIENT GREECE

c. 6000 B.C. First settlements on Greek island of Crete

c. 3000 B.C. Minoan culture arises on Crete

c. 1450 B.C. Mycenaeans take over Minoan settlements while building their own palaces in southern Greece

c. 1200–1100 B.C. End of Mycenaean culture, beginning of Dark Age in Greece

c. 1000–850 B.C. Founding of first Greek settlements in Ionia

700's B.C. Rise of city-states in Greece and founding of new settlements outside Greece

c. 650 B.C. First Greek law code is written in the settlement of Locris

c. 594 B.C. Solon introduces laws that help build **democracy** in Athens

508 B.C. Cleisthenes expands democracy in Athens

c. 500 B.C. Athens and Sparta emerge as strongest of the city-states

400's B.C. "Golden Age" of drama in Athens

490 B.C. Greek forces defeat Persia at Marathon

480 B.C. In the battle of Thermopylae, Greek forces lose to Persia, but allow Greece to prepare for and win battle at the island of Salamis

464 B.C. Slaves revolt in Sparta

457 B.C. Pericles further expands democracy in Athens

431–404 B.C. Peloponnesian War between Athens and Sparta

334 B.C. Alexander the Great invades Persian Empire

326 B.C. Alexander's forces reach what is now India, spreading Greek culture across Central Asia

323 B.C. Death of Alexander; his generals soon split his new empire into separate kingdoms

WHAT DID THE GREEKS ACHIEVE?

Much of Western **culture** has its roots in ancient Greek **civilization** *(SIHV uh luh ZAY shuhn)*. Many modern ideas about art, politics, and science can be traced back to the Greeks.

Politics and Government

In many nations today, people choose their leaders through elections. Some voters also have the right to approve or reject new laws. A government that gives citizens the right to vote for leaders and create laws is called a **democracy** *(dih MOK ruh see)*. The roots of this form of government began in ancient Greece.

Several Greek **city-states** had democratic governments, but the government of Athens was the most advanced. Government, the Athenians believed, should be based on laws, not the decisions of only one or a few people, so they sought many people's input. This idea of "rule by law" remains an important principle today.

Lovers of Wisdom

An ancient Greek named Protagoras *(proh TAG uh ruhs)* believed each person had to decide for himself or herself what was right or true. Then, through debate and discussion, a group of people could create the best laws. The role of the individual in society interested Greek thinkers called **philosophers**. **Philosophy** *(fuh LOS uh fee)* comes from two Greek words meaning "love

▼ On a rocky hill called the Pnyx *(nihks)*, Athenian citizens met in the 500's and 400's B.C. to vote on important issues facing the city. From a platform on the hill, a citizen could speak to several thousand people at once. These crowds sat on benches or on the ground.

of wisdom." Some Greek philosophers studied the stars, animal life, and how the human body works. Others described **ethics**—the nature of right and wrong actions or ideas. People still study ancient Greek philosophers to help them understand how human beings can live the best possible life.

Great Art

The individual was at the center of some of Greece's greatest art. Poets and writers explored human emotions and relationships. Greek sculptors learned how to show people as they really looked, with emotions and body movements. Painters also gained these skills.

The Greeks also excelled in architecture. They had certain building styles called **orders**. Each order called for a certain type and number of columns. Ancient Greek column styles and building design styles are still used today.

ANCIENT WONDERS

Five ancient Greek works are among the so-called Seven Wonders of the Ancient World. The tomb of the ruler Mausolus (*maw SOH luhs*), in Asia Minor, stood about 150 feet (46 meters) tall and featured a huge base topped by 36 columns holding up a pyramid. The statue of Zeus at Olympia depicted the god on a throne. The gold-and-ivory figure stood about 43 feet (13 meters) high. A colossus (*kuh LOS uhs*), or huge statue, of the sun god Helios (*HEE lee os*) was built at the harbor of the island of Rhodes (*rohdz*). This bronze statue stood about 110 feet (34 meters) tall. Another of the Greek wonders was the **temple** for the goddess Artemis (*AHR tuh mihs*) at Ephesus (*EHF ih suhs*), in Asia Minor. The temple's foundation measured about 360 by 180 feet (110 by 55 meters) and was surrounded by 106 columns, each about 67 feet (20 meters) high. The last Greek wonder was a 440-foot- (134-meter-) tall lighthouse built in the harbor of Alexandria, Egypt, when Greeks ruled there during the 200's B.C. Unfortunately, all of these famous structures have been destroyed in the centuries since they were built. Only traces remain.

▶ Statues from the Temple of Zeus (*zoos*) at Olympia, which honored Zeus, ruler of the gods in Greek **mythology**. The temple, which dated from the 500's B.C., housed a huge statue of Zeus that was considered one of the Seven Wonders of the Ancient World.

THE FIRST GREEKS

Long before the glory of ancient Greece, other notable settlements arose around the Aegean Sea. About 8,000 years ago, people first settled on the eastern Mediterranean island of Crete. By about 3000 B.C., they began to gain wealth through overseas trade. The people who built this **civilization** are now called the Minoans *(mih NOH uhnz)*. The Minoans were named for a legendary king of Crete, Minos. Through their trade, the Minoans learned about art and architecture. Around 2000 B.C., they began to build large palaces.

The Mycenaeans

Around 1450 B.C., fires destroyed almost all the Minoan palaces and their surrounding towns in a short time, weakening the Minoan culture. Only the palace at Knossos *(kuh NOS uhs)* on Crete survived, and it was soon taken over by the Mycenaeans *(MY suh NEE uhnz)*, people who came from southern Greece. The Mycenaeans had first moved into that region around 2000 B.C. and built a city called Mycenae *(my SEE nee)*. They traded with the Minoans and adapted the Minoan writing system.

▼ A Minoan wall painting of a musical procession at Knossos on the island of Crete. The figure third from the right plays a stringed instrument called a lyre *(lyr)*.

Like the Minoans, the Mycenaeans became rich from trade and built large palaces. These palaces appeared across southern and central Greece. Also like the Minoans, the Mycenaeans saw most of their palaces destroyed by fire, starting around 1200 B.C. This caused surrounding villages to decline and be abandoned. Foreign invasions and wars may have added to the Mycenaeans' problems. By 1100 B.C., their civilization had collapsed.

Leaving the Dark Age

Historians call the centuries after the fall of the Mycenaeans the Dark Age of ancient Greece. People left many towns and villages to live in other regions. The Greeks created much simpler art than they had before, and the knowledge of writing was lost. But the Greeks made some progress during this dark time—they found better ways to make tools and weapons out of iron. The iron made them stronger and easier to care for than the older bronze weapons and tools.

The Dark Age began to end around 800 B.C., when **city-states** began to emerge. The remaining cities from Mycenaean times began to extend their rule over nearby farming villages. The Greeks also began writing again. The city-states soon began to develop the Greek **culture** that would become the basis of Western civilization.

▲ The Lion Gate, named for the two lions carved into the rock, led into the palace of Mycenae on Greece's Peloponnesian Peninsula. The gate is about 10 feet (3 meters) wide and 10 feet high.

UNCOVERING THE PAST

After the decline of the Minoans and Mycenaeans, much of the evidence of their culture was lost. For hundreds of years, scholars were unaware that the great Aegean cultures had actually existed. In the 1870's, a German businessman and amateur **archaeologist** *(AHR kee OL uh jihst)* named Heinrich Schliemann *(HYN rihkh SHLEE mahn)* began searching for evidence of the Mycenaeans. Guided by ancient Greek texts, Schliemann discovered the remains of the city of Troy in Asia Minor, which he believed to be the one described by the poet Homer. He also discovered the city of Mycenae. Although later archaeologists have questioned some of Schliemann's methods, he is recognized as being instrumental in the field of ancient Greek archaeology.

REACHING OUT TO THE WORLD

The lands of the Minoans, Mycenaeans, and later Greeks lacked many natural resources. They needed to trade overseas to get certain metals and other items. Luckily, living on islands and **peninsulas**, the Greeks were never far from the sea. They built ships to move people and goods all over the Mediterranean region. The Mycenaeans were the first to trade widely across the Mediterranean. Their ships brought goods to and from such places as Asia Minor (what is now eastern Turkey), Sicily, and Egypt.

▼ Major Greek settlements founded between 750 and 500 B.C. Some remain important cities today. Byzantium is the modern-day city of Istanbul, Turkey. Massalia is Marseille, France, and Neapolis, on the Italian peninsula, is the city of Naples.

EGYPT'S IMPORTANCE

The Greek tradition of trade with Egypt went back to the Minoans. Egypt was a source of grain and other goods. By the 600's B.C., the Greeks had a trading post in Egypt called Naucratis *(NAW kruht uhs)*. The Greeks, and the Minoans and Mycenaeans before them, did more than trade with the Egyptians. From them, the Greeks learned building skills, styles of art, and methods of warfare. Egyptian ideas on mathematics, religion, and **philosophy** also influenced later Greek thinkers. Egyptian influence can be seen in many ancient Greek statues, buildings, and **artifacts.**

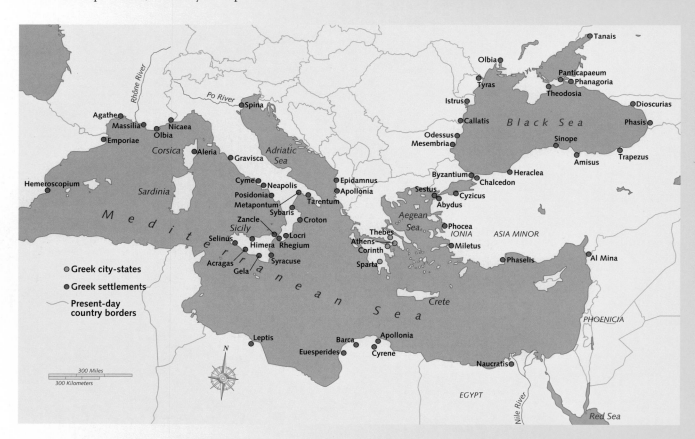

Types of Ships

The Mycenaean cargo ships had one sail. Around 500 B.C., the Greeks added a second mast and sail to their cargo ships. The second sail made the vessels easier to steer. Later ships had even more sails. A typical Greek ship carried from 100 to 200 tons (90 to 180 metric tons) of cargo.

The Greeks also built warships called galleys. They copied the design from the Phoenicians *(fuh NIHSH uhnz* or *fuh NEE shuhnz)*, who lived along the coast of what are now present-day Israel, Lebanon, and Syria. These galleys, also called biremes *(BY reemz)*, had a sail and two levels of oarsmen on each side of the ship. One set sat above the other. Later, the Greeks added a third level of oarsmen to each side of the ship, creating the trireme *(TRY reem)*. Extra rowers increased the ships' speed during battle.

Founding Settlements

In the Greek **city-states**, good farmland was hard to find. Neighboring cities sometimes fought each other over land. People also left Greece to settle overseas, where fertile land was more readily available. Some settlements had been founded as early as 1000 B.C. in the region called Ionia *(eye OH nee uh)* in Asia Minor. Beginning in the 700's B.C., the Greeks formed many new settlements along the coasts of the Aegean, Mediterranean, and Black Seas. These settlements were spread out over a huge area, ranging from as far west as what is now Spain to as far east as modern-day Russia. The largest settlements were in southern Italy and Sicily. The settlers usually kept some ties with the Greek city-state from which they had come.

The settlers traded with the local people as well as with other Greeks. Cargo ships carried crops, other goods, and people between the settlements and Greece. Well-made ships and excellent sailing skills brought the Greeks into contact with a world far beyond their homeland.

▲ Remains of a Greek ship dating from the 300's B.C. The wooden vessel was found in 1967 off the coast of Cyprus near the town of Kyrenia. It still held hundreds of jars of wine and almonds, which led **archaeologists** to conclude that it had been a trading ship.

WARS AND EMPIRES

By 500 B.C., Athens and Sparta were the two strongest Greek **city-states**. At this time, a great **empire** centered in Persia *(PUHR zhuh)*, the region that is modern-day Iran, stretched from India to the Greek cities of Ionia. When these Ionian cities rebelled against Persia in 499 B.C., Athens and another Greek city, Eretria *(eh REE tree uh)*, sent help. After the Persians had crushed the rebellion by 494 B.C., King Darius I *(duh RY uhs)* of Persia demanded that all the Greek cities pledge their loyalty to him. Athens, Sparta, and several others refused.

A Series of Wars

In 490 B.C., Persian troops headed for Athens. On the central Greek plain of Marathon *(MAIR uh thon)*, some 9,000 Athenian troops, along with 600 allies from other city-states, defeated a much larger Persian force. According to the historian Herodotus *(hih ROD uh tuhs)*, the Persians outnumbered the Greeks two to one, but modern historians doubt the accuracy of his claim. Darius's son Xerxes *(ZURK seez)* became king, and in 480 B.C. he led an even larger invasion of Greece. Xerxes managed to destroy much of Athens, but the Greeks won the war.

▲ An ancient seal imprinted with the type of warship the Greeks used in their conflicts with the Persians. In ancient times, seals—usually melted and congealed beeswax—indicated that documents were official and secured them from prying eyes. The imprint of the seal could be left on paper, clay, or metal.

Although Athens and Sparta were allied against Persia, they soon began fighting each other. During the 470's B.C., Athens founded its own empire. Its growing power worried Sparta, and in 431 Sparta launched the Peloponnesian War against Athens. The war's name comes from the Peloponnesus, the **peninsula** where Sparta is located. The war proceeded through several phases before Sparta defeated Athens in 404.

The Rise of Alexander

The kingdom of Macedonia *(mas uh DOH nyuh or mas uh DOH nee uh)* developed in northern Greece. The Macedonians were greatly influenced by the southern Greeks; the Macedonian leaders could read and write the Greek language. During the 330's B.C., Macedonia conquered the city-states of southern Greece. Alexander, the ruler of Macedonia, then led Greek and Macedonian soldiers into Asia. He defeated the Persian ruler Darius III and won control of his empire, which stretched from Egypt to India. Greek influence then spread throughout the old Persian Empire.

▼ Greek soldiers—armed with shields and short swords strapped across their chests—train with spears as depicted on a vase painting from the 400's B.C.

A Heroic Battle

A key battle in the second Greek-Persian war took place at a narrow strip of land between the mountains and the sea called Thermopylae *(thuhr MOP uh lee)*. Although they were outnumbered, the Greeks fought bravely. After two days of fighting, the Persians found a way to attack the Greeks from the rear, and most of the Greek defenders fled. A small force of Spartans and other Greeks, under the leadership of the Spartan King Leonidas *(lee ON ih duhs)*, stayed to fight. They were all killed, but they delayed the Persians long enough for a Greek navy to prepare for battle. Those ships defeated the Persians at the island of Salamis *(SAL uh mihs* or *SAH lah MEES)*. Leonidas and his soldiers became famous symbols of Spartan bravery and devotion to duty.

RULERS

A marble statue of Leonidas, who became king of Sparta around 489 B.C. He led the Spartan and other Greek soldiers who died heroically fighting the Persians at the Battle of Thermopylae in 480 B.C.

Through the centuries, the ancient Greeks lived under different forms of government. Leaving the Dark Age, most cities had kings. Wealthy men from the most important families sometimes gave the kings advice. These rich landowners called themselves aristoi *(AR uh stoy)*, or "best men." The English word aristocrat *(uh RIHS tuh krat)* comes from the word *aristoi*. Around 750 B.C., the aristocrats began taking control of the city governments. They created a form of government called an **oligarchy** *(OL uh GAHR kee)*, which means "rule by the few."

Tyrants

In some **city-states**, one aristocrat sometimes challenged the power of the oligarchy by illegally taking control of the government. This person was called a **tyrant** *(TY ruhnt)*. The word is still used today to describe a cruel leader. But in Greece, tyrants often won the support of some people. The tyrants gave them land and built important new public buildings. For example, Polycrates *(puh LIHK ruh TEEZ)*, a tyrant who ruled the island of Samos *(SAY mos or SAM ohs)* during the 540's B.C., built a **temple** and many other public works. Tyrants often tried to pass on their power to their sons. But the Greeks usually grew tired of one-man rule, and the aristocrats were often able to take back power.

Democracies

In Athens and several other cities, the oligarchies developed into **democracies**. In Athens, the process started around 594 B.C. with an aristocrat named Solon *(SOH luhn or SOH lon)*. He made the first laws that gave poor Athenians legal rights and gave more citizens a role in the government. Other aristocrats who followed him helped to shape democracy. These included Cleisthenes *(KLYS thuh neez)* and Pericles *(PEHR uh KLEEZ)*. In 457 B.C., Pericles changed the law so that any citizen could hold public

CLEISTHENES: BUILDER OF DEMOCRACY

Following the rule of a tyrant, Cleisthenes in 508 B.C. helped create a new democratic government in Athens. He allowed all male citizens to vote, and he created a 500-member **boule** *(BOO lee)*, or government council. Any male citizen could be selected to serve on this council, which ran the city's daily affairs. Members were chosen at random from citizens living in the city. Pericles, Cleisthenes's great-nephew, built on his uncle's reforms.

office. Several city-states drafted **constitutions**, written records of the fundamental principles according to which a nation, state, or group is governed. Under the constitution of Athens, male citizens could vote on laws, decide government policies, and elect generals during wartime. Democracy in Athens, however, was limited. Female citizens did not take part; neither did slaves or foreigners who lived in the city. The foreigners were called **metics** *(MEHT ihkz)*. Even without political rights, some metics became important members of Athenian society.

▶ A marble Roman copy of a Greek bust of Pericles, dating from the 100's B.C. Before beginning his career in government, Pericles was educated by some of the greatest thinkers in Athens. During the 30 years that he headed the Athenian government, the city paid salaries to its public officials for the first time and any male citizen gained the right to hold any office. The "Age of Pericles," as his rule came to be called, symbolized all that was highest in the art and science of the ancient world.

SOLDIERS

In ancient Greece, wars gave men a chance to prove their bravery and serve the city. In early times, Mycenaean chieftains and the best warriors fought each other in duels—one man against another. The regular soldiers threw javelins or fired arrows at each other. As the **city-states** grew, they raised larger armies. These armies included cavalry—soldiers on horseback—and archers. But the most powerful part of the Greek army was the infantry, or foot soldiers. The best of these infantry fighters were called **hoplites** *(HOP lytz)*. About half of the infantry consisted of these well-armed soldiers.

Hoplites

Hoplites fought using both long spears and short swords. They protected themselves with round shields. The weapons and gear these soldiers carried were called hopla, leading to the name hoplite. Rows of hoplites marched tightly together, creating a unit called a **phalanx** *(FAY langks* or *FAL angks)*. In battle, two opposing phalanxes marched toward each other and fought until one side fled in defeat.

▲ A phalanx of hoplites head into battle in a vase painting from the 500's B.C. Over the centuries, hoplite armor was made heavier and stronger. Bronze replaced softer materials, such as leather, and a thin layer of bronze also covered the hoplites' shields.

▶ A soldier on horseback in a **relief** sculpture from the 300's B.C. Cavalry troops were an especially important element in the army of Alexander the Great.

In most city-states, most able male citizens were expected to fight whenever there was a war. Wealthy farmers and traders had the most to lose if their city-state lost a battle, so they made up a large part of the army. They could also afford to buy weapons and armor. These soldiers had slaves who helped carry their weapons and supplies. Poorer citizens fought with lighter or no armor and used such simple weapons as slingshots. Because hoplites were so important to the army, they played a key role in the local governments. If they demanded more **democracy** or supported a **tyrant**, then the **oligarchy** paid attention. The leaders knew they had to keep their best soldiers happy. By the 400's B.C., however, the city-states were often hiring foreign soldiers to fight for them, meaning fewer citizens had to fight.

Sparta

Sparta was unique among the Greek city-states, as it was the only one with a permanent army. At age 7, young boys left home to begin training as soldiers. They were placed into units called companies. The bravest boy in each company was chosen as the captain, and the other boys had to obey his orders.

As young men, the soldiers served as a kind of police force for Sparta. At age 30, they were given their full rights as citizens. Soldiers were expected to serve in the military until age 60. In return for their service, the soldiers received land from the government, which was farmed by slaves. Sparta's soldiers were considered the best in Greece.

SPARTA AT WAR

All the Greeks valued bravery in battle, but especially the Spartans. According to legend, a Spartan mother gave her son his shield telling him to return from battle "either with it or on it," as Spartans who died in battle were often carried home on their shields. In other words, Spartans were expected to fight to the death and never run away. In this quote, a Spartan poet describes how Spartans should fight: "Stay, young men, shoulder to shoulder; do not turn in flight or be afraid…and never shrink when you face the foe. And do not leave your elders, whose knees are no longer nimble, fallen on the ground."

ARTISANS AND MERCHANTS

To the Greeks, owning and farming land was the best way to make a living. The wealthy looked down on people who made things with their hands. But the Greeks relied on skilled **artisans** *(AHR tuh zuhnz)* to provide many of the goods they needed for daily life, such as pottery, clothing, and metal goods. Certain cities were known for the skills of a particular type of artisan. Corinth, for example, was famous for the jewelry produced there. Megara *(MEHG uh ruh)*, not far from Athens, was known for its weavers and fine wool. Artisans in Athens crafted popular styles of red and black pottery featuring scenes from daily life.

An Artisan's Life

Artisans might work by themselves in small shops attached to their houses. People with similar skills tended to work and live near each other. Other artisans, particularly slaves,

▼ The first **agoras** *(AG uhr uhz)*, or central squares in Greek **city-states,** were land set aside for public assemblies. Over time, agoras became centers of commerce as well, where a variety of merchants would sell their wares. Most agoras had **stoas** *(STOH uhz)*. A stoa was a long outdoor hallway, closed on one side and covered with a roof.

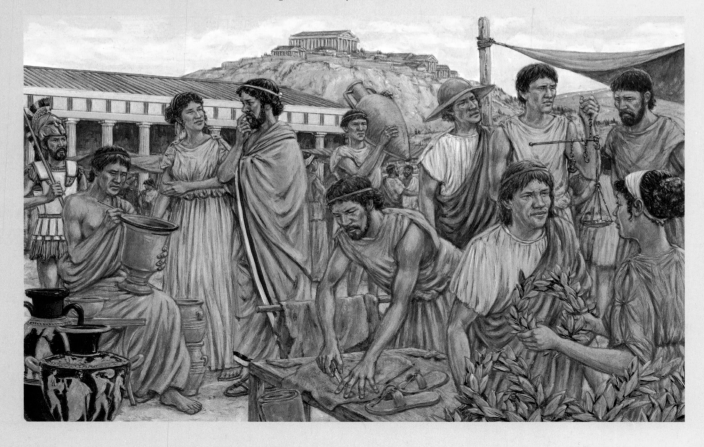

An ancient Athenian silver coin featuring a statue of Athena, the city's goddess, and her sacred bird, the owl. The coin was worth four drachma *(DRAK muh)*, the basic unit of money in ancient Athens. In the 1830's, Greece reintroduced the drachma as its official currency. It was in use until it was replaced by the euro in 2002.

worked in factories that could employ more than 100 workers. One of the larger factories made shields for soldiers. Laws restricted the ownership of land by **metics**, so many of them also became involved in making goods for sale. Many artisans took pride in their skills and made a good living with their hands.

Merchants

Merchants sold the goods made by Greek and foreign artisans. Some had their own shops; others set up booths in public areas. The stores included simple food-and-wine shops and banks where people could borrow money. Merchants worked under the watchful eye of city inspectors. These officials made sure the merchants used accurate weights and scales, so that they did not cheat their customers. The inspectors also made sure that merchants paid their taxes and that coins were real. Some people put thin layers of silver over cheap bronze coins, to try to fool others into thinking the coins were solid silver.

THE AGORA
Every Greek city had a central, open area called the agora. Many important public buildings lined the agora, and merchants tried to get as close to it as they could, so that they could attract the most customers. Like today's malls, the agora featured a variety of shops in one location. The agora, however, was more than a shopping center—people met there to discuss politics, **philosophy,** and business, or to gossip about their neighbors.

WOMEN

In ancient Greece, the lives of most women were focused on the home. Girls were taught that they should marry, have children, and take care of the house. A father had legal control over his daughters until they married. Then, the women's husbands took control of their lives. Most Greek men valued women because of their role as mothers and wives. Yet some also thought women were too emotional and might act without thinking—another reason for men to carefully watch their actions.

For female citizens, staying away from strangers was seen as proper behavior. In many Greek homes, women had their rooms on the top floors of the house. They did not enter the room set aside for the men to have dinner with friends. But women moved freely through the rest of the house and did many things outside it. Wealthy women, who had servants and slaves to do chores, took time to visit friends or relatives. Other women left the home to get water and to buy and sell goods. Women also went out to attend religious events.

A Woman's Duties

Along with household duties, women had several other roles. They spun thread and wove cloth to make clothes for their families. The poorest women often had to take jobs outside the home. They worked in shops or as servants to the wealthy. Some ran inns or worked outside their homes making cloth.

▶ A young Greek woman places clothes into a chest in a **relief** sculpture from the 400's B.C. Women controlled the making of cloth and clothing far back into Greek history. Greek legends suggest that even wealthy women wove cloth, rather than having servants do it for them.

Women also took part in **rituals**, or religious ceremonies. As priestesses, they performed the rituals connected to goddesses and some gods. The ceremonies were often held in **temples**. In some cases, only women could enter the temples.

Women in Sparta

Life for women in Sparta was very different from that in other parts of Greece. As girls, they went to schools run by the government and played sports, two things other Greek girls did not do. As they grew up, Spartan women were expected to have children, preferably sons, so Sparta would have more soldiers. The women were not expected to work outside the home, and they had slaves to do household chores. Female citizens of Sparta had more independence than women in other **city-states**.

FOR WOMEN ONLY

One Greek religious festival was for married women only. Thesmophoria *(thez moh FAWR ee uh)* was a three-day event that honored the goddesses Demeter *(dih MEE tuhr)* and Persephone *(puhr SEHF uh nee)*. The ceremony was held in many cities. In Athens, women headed to the Pnyx, the hill where men held political assemblies. For one day, the women went without food to show their devotion to the gods. They also amused the gods by shouting insults at each other. Both of these acts were meant to win the gods' favor, so that they would give the Greeks good crops. In addition to this important religious role, Thesmophoria also gave women time to leave their homes and enjoy the company of other women.

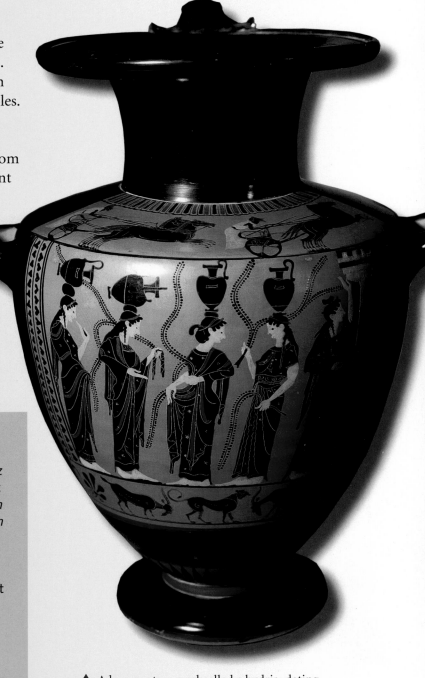

▲ A large water vessel called a hydria, dating from the 500's B.C., is decorated with women carrying the same kind of jug on their heads. In ancient Greek cities, a daily chore for most women was collecting water from public fountains and carrying it home to their families.

FARMERS

▲ A **terra cotta** sculpture of a farmer plowing behind a team of oxen, dating from the 500's B.C. In Athens in this period, one class of citizens consisted of men who owned a team of oxen and enough land to annually produce a certain quantity of grain. These farmers made up most of the **hoplite** forces.

Greece is a rocky, mountainous land, so farmland is limited. Rainfall is scarce in some regions. Sunshine is plentiful, however, and the ancient Greeks managed to raise a variety of crops and livestock. Many Greeks had ties to the land, either owning it, farming it, or both. About 90 percent of the people played some part in farming. Most farms were small, with the food produced going to feed the household. This included the landowner, his family, and any slaves he might own. A few wealthy landowners had farmlands scattered over a wide area, and male slaves did most of the work.

THE POMEGRANATE

The ancient Greeks considered the pomegranate *(POM gran iht* or *POM uh gran iht)* a symbol of marriage, and it played a role in the **myth** of Persephone. The goddess was kidnapped by Hades *(HAY deez)*, the god of the dead. Her mother, Demeter, was the goddess of agriculture and fertility. Demeter was angry and refused to let crops grow until Hades returned Persephone. However, Persephone had eaten pomegranate seeds while in the underworld, meaning she was married to Hades. Zeus, the ruler of the gods, arranged a solution under which Persephone had to stay with Hades for four months each year, but lived with Demeter for the rest of the year. Demeter was sad while Persephone was away, and crops did not grow. For the ancient Greeks, this explained why winter occurred.

Riches from the Land

The climate of Greece was good for growing wheat and barley. Greek farmers also raised olives, figs, beans, nuts, and grapes. Some olives were turned into olive oil, and grapes were turned into wine. Families also had small vegetable gardens.

Greek farmers raised livestock for food and clothing. Sheep and goats grazed on hilly land not suitable for farming. Both were raised for their meat; sheep also provided wool for clothing, and the goats gave milk that was turned into cheese. Pigs and fowl were other common livestock animals. Only the richest farmers raised cattle and horses, which needed much more grazing land than did sheep and goats. Cattle were raised for their meat, and their skins were turned into leather. Unless they were very poor, farmers also usually had mules or oxen to pull plows.

Ensuring Good Harvests

Crops need **nutrients** *(NOO tree uhntz)*. Most of these come from chemicals in the soil. Over time, nutrients must be returned to the soil. In some years, Greek farmers would not grow crops on part of their land. Sheep and goats would then graze on whatever grass grew there. The animals' manure added nutrients back to the soil. The Greeks also saved the waste from other animals—and from themselves—to spread over their farmland.

◀ A vase called an amphora *(AM fuhr uh)*, dating from the 500's B.C., is decorated with farm workers using rods to beat olives from a tree. Amphoras were used to store olive oil and wine. Traders often used less decorative examples to transport olive oil and wine over long distances. Many have been found intact in the holds of sunken ships.

SLAVES

Slavery existed long before the Greek **city-states** rose to power. After a war, defeated enemies were forced to work on farms. The Greeks kept up this tradition, and they also bought slaves captured in foreign lands. Only the poorest families did not own at least one slave, and the rich might have dozens, or even thousands. They would rent out some of these slaves to others for various jobs. During the 400's B.C., Athens alone had tens of thousands of slaves.

A Slave's Life

Slaves performed a wide range of duties. Female slaves lived with the free women of a household and worked next to them spinning and weaving. Male slaves also did household chores and ran errands for their masters. Some worked as farmers or **artisans**. The cities owned slaves as well. Some helped public officials run the government. The worst job for the city-owned slaves was mining silver, a very dangerous and difficult job.

Slaves were the property of their masters, who were free to beat them, though masters were not supposed to kill them for no reason. Slaves in some parts of Greece (though not in Athens) had some legal rights. A law code found at Gortyn (*gawr TEEN*), a city-state in Crete, outlined punishments for some crimes committed against

◀ A carved stone Greek funerary stele (*STEE lee*), a memorial or gravestone, dating from the 500's B.C. The work shows two women, one seated, the other, possibly a slave, holding a baby. Female slaves often helped Greek mothers raise children.

◀ A sculpture of Aesop *(EE sop)*, who lived from about 620 to 565 B.C. and whose fables, or stories with morals, are still widely read and told today. Although little is certain about his life, experts know that he was for some time a slave on the island of Samos. This bust portrays him as a handsome man, but some accounts describe him as ugly and deformed.

them. Some masters treated their household slaves well. Slaves earned money for their work, especially as artisans, and they could hold important jobs, such as banker, doctor, and teacher. Some slaves saved enough to buy their freedom from their masters or won freedom by serving as soldiers.

THE REBELLION OF 464

A powerful earthquake struck Sparta around 465 B.C. In the resulting chaos, some helots from Messenia rebelled against their masters. Fighting between these helots and Spartans lasted for at least four years before the Messenians finally gave up. They were allowed to leave the Peloponnesus, as long as they promised never to return. If they did, they would be enslaved again. Many of the surviving helots settled in a town under Athens' control. About a century later, Messenia finally won its independence from Sparta, with help from Thebes.

The Helots of Sparta

Early in its history, Sparta began conquering neighboring lands. Some of the people they defeated kept some independence, though they had to fight for Sparta during wars. A larger group, from an area of the Peloponnesus called Messenia *(muh SEE nee uh)*, became slaves known as **helots** *(HEHL uhtz)*. Other helots came from the regions directly around Sparta. The helots farmed for the Spartan citizens. They greatly outnumbered the Spartans, who feared the helots would act together and rebel. Each year, the Spartans declared war against the helots. This way, young men could kill helots without breaking the law against murder. The Spartans first spied on the helots and then they killed any who seemed like they might become leaders of a slave revolt.

Laws, Crime, and Punishment

In ancient Greece, each city had its own set of laws and form of government. Zaleucus *(za LOO kuhs)*, of the colony of Locris *(LOH kruhs or LOK ruhs)* in Italy, is said to have created the first written Greek law code around 650 B.C. The Gortyn law code was written during the 400's B.C. but was probably based on much older laws. Athens had such important lawgivers as Draco *(DRAY koh)* and Solon.

The Athenians created the model of democratic government. It had three branches, or parts. The assembly of all citizens and the **boule** formed the **legislative** *(LEHJ ihs LAY tihv)* branch. Any citizen could propose a law in the assembly. The second branch had various officials who carried out the laws. The third, **judicial** *(joo DIHSH uhl)*, branch, was made up of the courts. Greek citizens served on **juries** to decide if laws followed the city's **constitution** and if accused lawbreakers were innocent or guilty.

Crimes and Trials

The first recorded laws in Athens made murder a crime. Stealing was also illegal, as was taking actions that harmed the city. Insulting or hitting a fellow citizen was also against the law. Athens did not have police who tracked down criminals. Instead, citizens accused each other of breaking the law. For murders, usually only the victim's relatives could bring charges against the killer. But other citizens could accuse someone of murder if the victim did not have relatives.

For trials, jurors were selected by chance from a large group of citizens. A trial had at least 201 jurors, and some had more than 1,000. Criminals and their accusers both argued their case to the

◄ The law code from the city of Gortyn on Crete was carved into the walls of a public building for all citizens to see. The laws deal with such things as the rights of citizens and slaves, marriage, and divorce. In some cases, the code includes fines people must pay if they break the laws.

Ostracism

The Athenians had a fear of **tyrants**, and once a year citizens could vote to exile for a 10-year period anyone who seemed a danger to **democracy.** The names of the potential tyrants were recorded on a piece of pottery called an ostrakon *(OS truh kon)*. The word is the root of the English word ostracism *(OS truh sihz uhm)*, the act of forcing or leaving someone out of a group. The ostrakon at right has "Themistocles" *(thuh MIHS tuh KLEEZ)* on it. Themistocles honorably served in the Athenian government in the 490's B.C. and was a commander during the second war with Persia in 480. Themistocles was exiled around 470 B.C. for alleged disloyalty to Athens.

jurors. Good public speakers usually had an advantage in winning their cases. People could also hire others to write speeches for them. Surviving speeches give us clues about the Athenian legal system. Witnesses also appeared, describing what they knew about the crime or the accused. Jurors then voted in secret to decide whether the accused was guilty or not. A vote of at least half the jurors plus one decided the result.

Punishment

The Athenians had a range of punishments. The guilty might have to pay a fine or lose some legal rights. Other criminals were exiled—forced to leave the city—or executed. Few people spent time in jail, as jails were costly to build and run.

BELIEFS AND GODS

To help understand their history and the world around them, the Greeks created **myths**. These stories described the actions of the gods and goddesses thought to control the world. These powerful beings ruled over human actions and the natural world. The gods looked and acted like people, but they had special powers and never died. Gods could change their form and predict events.

The Major Gods

The Greeks believed that the 12 most powerful gods lived on Mount Olympus, the highest mountain in Greece. Each of these gods, as well as the lesser gods, had certain interests or powers. For example, Zeus, the most powerful god, ruled over heaven and the sky. He made lightning appear by throwing thunderbolts. His brother Poseidon *(puh SY duhn)* was god of the sea and earthquakes. Apollo *(uh POL oh)*, a son of Zeus, was god of the sun and also of medicine, music, and poetry, among other things. Apollo's twin sister Artemis was goddess of hunting and the moon. According to Greek myth, Athena, the goddess of warfare and wisdom, was born from the head of Zeus, full-grown and dressed in armor. The **city-state** of Athens was named after, and dedicated to, Athena.

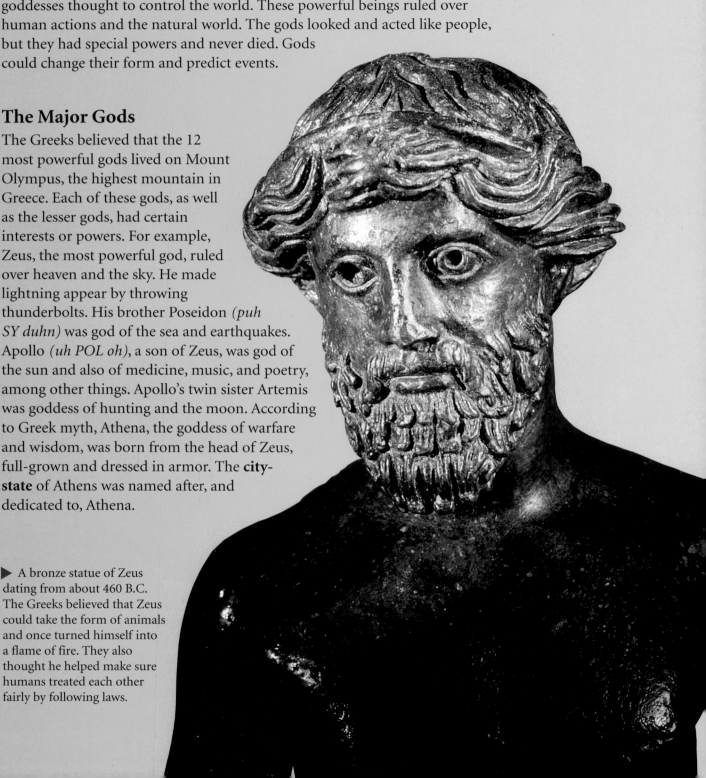

▶ A bronze statue of Zeus dating from about 460 B.C. The Greeks believed that Zeus could take the form of animals and once turned himself into a flame of fire. They also thought he helped make sure humans treated each other fairly by following laws.

THE TROJAN WAR

The Trojan War is one of the most famous events in Greek literature, the inspiration behind many Greek epic poems and plays. The 10-year-long war began after Paris, the son of the king of Troy, kidnapped Helen, a Greek queen and the most beautiful woman in the world. The greatest Greek heroes, including Achilles *(uh KIHL eez)* and Odysseus *(oh DIHS ee uhs)*, sailed to Troy and attacked the city. In one battle, shown above in a painting on a krater *(KRAY tuhr;* a type of jar), made about 530 B.C., the two sides fight over the dead body of a friend of Achilles. The gods disguised themselves as warriors and joined the war, some helping the Greeks and others helping the Trojans. Eventually the Greeks built a huge wooden horse, placed it outside the walls of Troy, and pretended to leave. However, Greek warriors were hiding inside. The Trojans thought that the horse was a gift, signifying the end of the war, and brought it into the city. The Greek soldiers crept out of the horse that night, opened the gates of the city, and let in the rest of the Greek army. They rescued Helen, burned Troy, and slaughtered most of the Trojans. Historians are not sure if the war actually took place or if stories about it mix facts with fiction.

The Greeks thought that the gods played an active role in human events. The gods might answer prayers for help. But if humans upset the gods, they became angry and could cause illness or natural disasters. Each Greek city-state had its own god or goddess thought to protect it and its citizens.

Recording the Myths

Some of what historians know about ancient Greek myths comes from the **epic** poetry of Hesiod *(HEE see uhd* or *HEHS ee uhd)* and Homer. During the 700's B.C., these writers composed long poetic tales about the gods and their actions. Over the centuries, many other artists and writers used the myths as subjects for their works. The names of the gods and versions of their stories remain part of the literature of Western **civilization.**

CEREMONIES

The Greeks worshipped the major gods of Olympus, lesser gods, demigods, and heroes. Each god was honored at a holy place called a **sanctuary** *(SANGK chu EHR ee)*. The sanctuary included an **altar** where sacrifices were made and might also have a **temple**. Inside the temple stood a statue of the temple's god or goddess.

Each sanctuary had priests or priestesses who took care of the space and any items left there. Anyone could perform some **rituals**, such as offering food or drink to the gods, but the priests and priestesses watched over these ceremonies. Other rituals were performed only by the priests and priestesses.

▼ The sanctuary of Apollo at Delphi was located near Mount Parnassus *(pahr NAS uhs)*. Ancient Greece's most famous oracle was located at Delphi and was often consulted on major political matters. Many **city-states** and colonies made donations and built tributes to the Delphic oracle.

ORACLES

At many sanctuaries there were **oracles**, people who were thought to be able to speak to a particular god or goddess. Many oracles were women. The most famous oracle was for Apollo at Delphi. The sanctuary was located at what the Greeks believed was the center of the world. They called this the omphalos *(OM fuh luhs)*, or navel. A dozen different cities helped run the sanctuary, and even non-Greeks came seeking predictions. People asked the female oracle, called the Pythia *(PIHTH ee uh)*, a question. She gave the god's response in strange words, and priests then tried to make sense of what she said. The painting on the vase at right shows the Pythia with King Aegeus *(EE jee uhs* or *EE joos)* of Athens, who is seeking her help. **Archaeologists** suggest that gases coming from the Earth at Delphi put the Pythia into a trance.

Sacrifices

The most important ritual at a Greek religious ceremony was making a sacrifice.
An animal, such as a bull, goat, sheep, or pig, was sacrificed on a temple's altar. The animal was then roasted for everyone to eat. Some parts were left behind as gifts to the god. Wine was also poured on the altar for the god. In some sacrifices, animals were not killed, and people left behind such things as bread or locks of hair.

Burial Ceremonies

The Greeks had various ideas about the afterlife—what happened to people after they died. But they agreed that funeral ceremonies had to follow certain rituals, so the dead would be at peace. Friends and relatives came to mourn, or express their sadness, before the body was buried. Sometimes the dead person was first cremated before burial. At the cemetery, the mourners placed coins and daily items in the dead person's grave, thinking the items would be needed in the afterlife. After the burial, relatives continued to bring food or drink to the grave to honor the dead person. These visits usually took place on the anniversary of the death and on holidays.

HEALTH AND MEDICINE

▲ Ruins of the asclepeion on Cos. This Greek island was the second-most important center for medicine in the Greek world. The most important was Epidaurus (*EHP ih DAWR uhs*), where the main sanctuary for Asclepius, the god of healing, was located.

When the flu hit or their bodies ached, the Greeks turned to the gods for help. Asclepius (*as KLEE pee uhs*), a son of Apollo, was the god of healing, and he received most of the requests for aid. Asclepius's symbol, a rod with a snake wrapped around it, is still used as a symbol for many health and medical organizations.

A GREEK "HOSPITAL"

Most Greek towns had **sanctuaries** for Asclepius, called asclepeions *(as KLEE pee onz)*. Sick people stayed at these early forms of hospitals, praying and offering sacrifices to the god. The patients also rested and sometimes bathed in clean water. Members of their families could stay in rooms at the sanctuary. The most important part of the treatment came at night. The Greeks believed that Asclepius appeared in the patients' dreams and told them what was wrong and how it could be cured. In the morning, priests at the sanctuary explained the dream and began treating the patient.

The Greeks thought that snakes had healing powers. In ancient Greece, the sick also sometimes wore charms or chanted special words thought to have magical healing powers.

Hippocrates

During the 400's B.C., a physician named Hippocrates *(hih POK ruh TEEZ)* on the island of Cos became one of the first Greeks to think of medicine as a science, and not part of religion. Hippocrates saw that people who prayed to the gods for help had about the same chance of being cured as those who did not pray. He believed that something in nature caused disease and that natural cures, not prayer, could treat it.

Hippocrates thought that the human body was made of four main liquids, which he called *humors.* If these liquids were not balanced correctly, people became ill. He also thought doctors should learn from the writings of other doctors and from what they observed in their patients. Hippocrates believed that in many cases, the body could cure itself over time.

Lasting Influence

Modern doctors know Hippocrates' idea about humors was wrong. But the Greek doctor paved the way for a new kind of medicine. People slowly began to trust science to cure sickness. Doctors after him would carefully record their patients' problems and the treatments they used. They would learn from each other. Doctors still take an oath named for Hippocrates, which states their desire to do everything they can to heal and not hurt their patients.

▶ A Roman marble copy of a Greek portrait bust of Hippocrates. Hippocrates is thought to have written about 80 medical works, though his name was not on them. A later physician named Galen *(GAY luhn)* called Hippocrates the father of medicine and spread his ideas about the body's four humors.

FESTIVALS

Sacrifices and religious **rituals** were often part of the events held during religious festivals. These festivals honored the god or goddess that looked after a particular city. Smaller villages held their own festivals for local gods. The festivals had their roots in ancient celebrations that marked the changing of the seasons.

A typical festival featured a procession—a parade of people. The festivalgoers ate, drank, and enjoyed different forms of entertainment. Speakers recited the works of Homer, and people sang and danced. Musicians played flutes and such stringed instruments as the lyre and the kithara *(KIHTH uhr uh)*. In Athens, at the yearly festival for the god Dionysus *(DY uh NY suhs)*, actors performed plays, and they and the writers won prizes for the best work. At other festivals, athletes also competed for prizes.

▼ The Parthenon, which stands atop the Acropolis in Athens, was completed in 432 B.C. Honoring Athena, the temple originally held a 30-foot- (9-meter-) tall, gold and ivory statue of Athena, patron goddess of Athens. The city's procession for Athena ended at the Parthenon.

The Panhellenic Festivals

The most important festivals were panhellenic *(PAN huh LEHN ihk),* that is, open to all Greeks. People came from across Greece to worship and celebrate at these events. The festivals helped create a sense of a shared **culture** among the **city-states.** The athletic games held at four of these festivals were the largest in the Greek world. They took place either every two or every four years. The oldest was the festival at Olympia, to honor Zeus. Its games inspired the modern Olympics. The Nemean *(nih MEE uhn or NEE mee uhn)* Games also honored Zeus. The Isthmian *(IHS mee uhn)* Games, held near Corinth, honored Poseidon. The Pythian Games, held at Delphi, honored Apollo.

Other Festivals

Some festivals were only for certain people or marked special events in daily life. Athenian slaves had Kronia *(KROH nee uh),* a day when they feasted and moved freely throughout the city. The Apaturia *(ap uh TOO ree uh)* festival marked the day when infant boys were shown to a sort of extended family group called a phratry *(FRAY tree).* One festival, called the Anthesteria *(an thehs TIHR ree uh),* celebrated the first drinking of new wine.

THE PANATHENAEA

Athens had several festivals to honor the goddess Athena, the guardian of the city. The largest, the greater Panathenaea *(PAN ath uh NEE uh),* was held every four years, with a smaller yearly festival marking her birthday. Rams and bulls were sacrificed to the goddess, and the citizens feasted on the meat. Young girls made a new dress, which they left at a statue of Athena at her **sanctuary.** The games at the Panathenaea were the only ones to have team sports, and winners received valuable prizes, rather than the simple wreaths awarded at other games.

▶ A krater, or jar, from the Greek settlement at Taras in the Puglia (or Apulia) region of southeastern Italy. The piece is decorated with figures participating in festival dancing. Dancing and music were important aspects of Greek religious festivals.

TEMPLES, TOMBS, AND OTHER STRUCTURES

Beginning in the 700's B.C., the Greeks began replacing wooden temples with brick or marble ones. The most famous of these is the Parthenon, a temple dedicated to Athena built on the Acropolis. Impressive temples to many other gods are found throughout Greece and the rest of the ancient Greek world.

Styles of Temples

The Greeks developed three major **orders**, or styles, for temples. Each used its own type of column and building details. The oldest and most common was the Doric *(DAWR ihk)* order. Its columns had no square base, and the buildings had simple decorations. Doric columns are noted for the pillowlike tablet at the capital (the decorative top). In general, the Greeks prized balance, harmony, and proportion in their buildings, and architects used set measurements and ratios for columns. A Doric column was usually from 5 to 7 times taller than the width of its lowest diameter. The columns on the Parthenon are Doric. The columns in the Ionic *(y ON ihk)* order were from 9 to 10 times taller than their lower diameters and featured more elaborate designs on the column itself as well as on the capital, which featured a scroll design. The third and most **ornate** order is the Corinthian *(kuh RIHN thee uhn)*, which became popular after the rule of Alexander the Great. The Corinthian capital is designed to look like the leaves of the acanthus *(uh KAN thuhs)* plant.

Tombs and Other Buildings

Wealthy Greeks sometimes built tombs to hold their remains. They featured statues on the outside and paintings on the inside. The most famous Greek tomb was built in the 300's B.C. for a ruler named Mausolus. Located in the city of Halicarnassus *(hal uh*

Types of Greek Columns

capital

base

Doric   Ionic   Corinthian

DECORATIVE TEMPLES

The ancient Greeks built complex and ornate temples. Many of the most famous of these were stone temples built during the 500's and 400's B.C. Temples consisted of an arrangement of columns around a long, inner chamber housing a statue to whom the temple was dedicated. On the front and rear of a temple, the columns held up a slab called an architrave *(AHR kuh trayv)*. Above the architrave rested the frieze *(freez)*, a horizontal band decorated with sculptures. Above the frieze rested a triangular piece called a pediment *(PEHD uh muhnt)*, which was filled with large, dramatic sculptures of many figures. Each side of the temple also had a decorated frieze. This form of architecture influenced later Roman temples, as well as such modern buildings in the classical style as the United States Supreme Court Building in Washington, D.C.

kahr NAS uhs) in Asia Minor, it stood about 150 feet (46 meters) tall and featured a huge base topped by 36 columns supporting a pyramid. The pyramid was surrounded by carved images created by some of the most skilled sculptors of the day. **Archaeologists** believe that a statue of Mausolus in a chariot probably stood atop the pyramid. The building became so famous that large tombs are now known as mausoleums *(MAW suh LEE uhmz)*. An earthquake destroyed the tomb in the A.D. 1200's.

The Greeks also constructed large public buildings, such as theaters and **stoas**. For theaters, stone seats were arranged in a half-circle on a hill, with the stage at the bottom. The largest theaters could hold up to 14,000 people and were built so that everyone could hear the actors. A stoa was a long outdoor hallway, closed on one side and covered with a roof. It was often lined with columns. Stoas held shops, and people met at them to hear lectures or argue legal cases.

A Typical Greek Temple

— pediment
— frieze
— architrave
— column

POTTERY, PAINTING, AND SCULPTURE

Greek artists were renowned for their pottery. These artists made everyday items out of clay, including vases, jugs, bowls, lamps, and jars. They then decorated them with intricate designs and paintings. Pottery offers some of the best examples of Greek painting styles, since many wall paintings have not survived.

Painting of All Kinds

Early Greek potters painted their work with shapes and lines. During the 600's B.C., they began showing scenes from **myths** or from daily life, such as animal hunts. A distinct style of pottery painting developed in Athens, featuring human figures in black or red. Battles, marriages, and feasts were sometimes shown, and **archaeologists** study this art to learn more about Greek life.

Some Greek artists also painted large works on the walls of buildings. Most that survive were made on the insides of tombs. Archaeologists know of other artworks that did not survive from descriptions made by ancient Roman writers. Greek painters tried to show human expressions, and some of their best works were later copied by Roman artists.

Sculpture

The Greeks learned sculpting skills from the Egyptians and other neighboring peoples. By the 600's B.C., they were making large sculptures, and they perfected ways of showing great human emotion and action. The artists also showed such fine details as the folds in clothing. Some statues were free-standing; others decorated the outsides of temples.

Greek sculptors made their works out of clay, wood, marble, and bronze. Few bronze sculptures remain today, because they were later melted down. Many Greek works are known because later Roman artists copied the statues in marble, which is much more durable. Later Greek sculptures in marble, such

THE KOUROS

One famous type of Greek statue, the **kouros** *(KOOR os)*, which is Greek for "young male," was common from the 600's to the late 400's B.C. The typical kouros showed a naked teenage boy with his left foot forward and his hands clenched by his side. The marble kouros shown here was created in the 500's B.C. Kouroi *(KOOR oy)* were often shown standing guard at **temples** and tombs. Kouroi were influenced by earlier sculptures from Egypt, but the Greeks made their statues more lifelike. A female version, called a kore *(KAWR ay* or *KAWR ee)*, showed a clothed teenage girl.

as *Winged Victory* (about 190 B.C.), which depicts Nike *(NY kee* or *NEE kay)*, the goddess of victory, and a statue of Aphrodite known as the *Venus de Milo (VEE nuhs duh MEE loh)* (about 130 B.C.), are renowned as some of the classical world's most important works.

▲ The *Winged Victory of Samothrace*, which dates from between 220 and 190 B.C., was discovered by a French amateur archaeologist in 1863. The 8-foot (2.4-meter) figure represents Nike, the goddess of victory, and was probably made to commemorate success in a sea battle.

LITERATURE

After the Dark Age, the Greeks created their first known literature, starting with **epic** poems. These poems were long tales of Greek heroes and gods. According to tradition, two of these, the *Iliad (IHL ee uhd)* and the *Odyssey (OD uh see)*, were composed by the poet Homer. The Iliad describes events during the Trojan War, and the Odyssey is about the journeys of the hero Odysseus *(oh DIHS ee uhs)* as he attempts to return to Greece after that war. Historians are not sure that Homer actually existed. Some think the poems he supposedly wrote were actually created by several different writers. After Homer, shorter poems became more common. These works often talked about the poet's thoughts and feelings.

Drama

The earliest Greek plays were performed at festivals for Dionysus, the god of wine. The Greeks originally sang and danced to honor him; then they began telling stories on a stage. The first of these were **tragedies**—stories, often based on **myths,** about people who faced difficult choices and came to an unhappy end. The "Golden Age" of Greek tragedy came in Athens during the 400's B.C. Aeschylus *(EHS kuh*

▼ An amphitheater at the site of the ancient city of Epidaurus is perhaps the best-preserved of ancient Greek theaters. The theater is famous for its sound quality, and performances are still held there.

luhs), Sophocles *(SOF uh KLEEZ)*, and Euripides *(yoo RIHP uh deez)* were the greatest playwrights of the day. Of the surviving Greek tragedies, all but one were written by these three playwrights. The Greeks also developed **comedy**. These stories often looked at the lives of average people or poked fun at people and issues of the day. Aristophanes *(AR ih STOF uh NEEZ)* was the best of the comic writers.

History

During the 400's B.C., Herodotus and Thucydides *(thoo SIHD ih DEEZ)* wrote the first Greek histories. Herodotus traveled throughout the Mediterranean region, gathering facts from people he met. Modern historians know that he sometimes recorded legends rather than true information. Thucydides is considered a more accurate historian, though he focused more on events from his own lifetime. Herodotus wrote about Greece's wars with Persia, and Thucydides addressed some events of the Peloponnesian War. Both writers showed that history could tell a good story while recording facts.

THE MASKS OF GREEK DRAMA

In Greek plays, men wearing masks played all the roles. The masks made it easier for them to perform many roles in the same play. Each mask represented a different role. Some masks had broad expressions for different emotions. They made it easier for people at the back of the theater to understand what characters were feeling. The masks may have also helped project an actor's voice to the distant seats. Two masks, one with a smiling face (comedy) and one with a sad face (tragedy), remain in use as symbols for the dramatic arts.

▼ A performer at the 2004 Olympic Games in Athens holds masks representing comedy and tragedy.

PHILOSOPHY

W hat is the nature of the universe? What is the purpose of human life? Greek **philosophers** wrestled with questions like these and shared their ideas with others. The first known Western philosophers lived in Miletus *(my LEET uhs* or *muh LEET uhs)*, in Asia Minor, during the 500's B.C. One of them, Thales *(THAY leez)*, emerged as the first major Greek thinker. He and other early Greek philosophers thought the gods did not influence events on Earth. They hoped to find the true cause of natural and human events through their senses, such as sight and hearing. Their explanations of the world were not always correct, but they led others to think even deeper about life and nature.

The Great Minds of Athens

During the 400's B.C., Athens became the center of learning in Greece. The first major philosopher in Athens was named Socrates *(SOK ruh TEEZ)*. Socrates asked his students many questions about what and how

THE DEATH OF SOCRATES

Socrates said that "The unexamined life is not worth living." In other words, people should always think about their actions and question their beliefs. However, some Greeks disliked Socrates's commenting on people and how they lived. Plato's *Apology of Socrates* describes how, in 399 B.C., Socrates was found guilty of "not believing in the gods the state believes in, and introducing different new divine powers; and also for corrupting the young" and was sentenced to die. Although Socrates felt the court's decision was unjust and he could have escaped, he felt morally obligated to accept his sentence. He drank a poison, hemlock, and faced death with courage.

▼ *The Death of Socrates* (1787) by French artist Jacques Louis David *(zhahk lwee dah VEED)*. Socrates reaches for the poison hemlock that will kill him. Plato, at the foot of the bed, faces away, resigned to his teacher's fate.

they thought. He wanted people to see for themselves that their ideas were not always right and that they often contradicted themselves. This teaching approach, of asking people to closely examine their thoughts, is called the Socratic method and is still used today.

Plato and Aristotle

Socrates's greatest student was named Plato *(PLAY toh)*. He wrote down many of his teacher's ideas in the form of dialogues. Plato also developed his own **philosophy**. He believed humans could not know the world through their senses. They could know the true nature of objects and ideas only through their minds.

Plato founded a school called the Academy on the outskirts of Athens. He and other teachers taught men—and some women—about philosophy and science. Plato's greatest student was named Aristotle. For several decades in the 300's B.C., Aristotle wrote on a wide range of subjects. He explored the natural world, art, and the stars and planets. He also created the field of logic, a system for proving that certain related facts are true. Aristotle also wrote about **ethics,** politics, and literature. The ideas of Socrates, Plato, and Aristotle are considered the foundation of Western philosophy and continue to influence modern philosophers.

◀ A marble bust of Aristotle—a Roman copy after a Greek bronze original by Lysippos from 330 B.C. The philosopher and scientist Aristotle is considered one of the most influential thinkers in Western civilization. His thoughts and discoveries in the fields of art, ethics, philosophy, politics, and science have remained influential for hundreds of years.

SCIENCE, MATH, AND TECHNOLOGY

The interest of the great Greek **philosophers** in the world and ways of thinking led to changes in science and mathematics. The Greek philosophers believed that the world had laws that were always true and that human beings could discover them by observing the world and using their minds.

Aristotle studied plants and animals, helping to create the science of biology. He grouped living things together based on their looks and habits. Hippocrates helped make medicine a science by observing patients' behavior and what helped them get better. Democritus (*dih MOK rih tuhs*) thought that the whole world was made up of tiny particles called atoms. Other Greeks rejected this, but his idea was later shown to be true.

Greeks and Mathematics

The Egyptians and other ancient people used numbers to count. The Greeks, however, went further in developing some branches of

▼ The Archimedean (*AHR kuh MEE dee uhn*) screw, or Archimedes screw, in an engraving from the early 1900's. The ancient Greek philosopher and scientist Archimedes invented the device, which is a screw inside an angled pipe that when turned by a handle allows water to be drawn upward.

mathematics. They tried to find relationships between numbers and how they applied to the world. Thales worked in geometry *(jee OM uh tree)*, the study of lines, angles, and curves. So did Pythagoras *(pih THAG uhr uhs)*, who taught that numbers were essential to all things. He formulated what is known as the *Pythagorean theorem (pih* THAG *uh REE uhn THEE uhr uhm)*, which explains the relationship between the lengths of the sides of a right-angled triangle. Euclid *(YOO klihd)*, who lived around 300 B.C., wrote a geometry textbook. He took accepted mathematical facts and used them to prove earlier ideas about geometry and solve problems.

Putting Knowledge to Use

The Greek scientists often worked on theorems and dealt with ideas. Archimedes *(*AHR *kuh MEE deez)* was one philosopher who used his knowledge in practical ways. He invented a type of pulley. This device uses small wheels and rope to help a person lift heavy objects. Archimedes also invented a large screw-shaped device for taking water out of a river. As the screw turned, its curving sides pulled up the water. The screw is still used today and is named for Archimedes.

▼ A marble bust of Pythagoras in a Roman copy of a Greek bronze from the 500's B.C. Although known as a mathematician, Pythagoras was also a philosopher and believed that Earth was spherical and that the sun, moon, and planets have movements of their own. Unlike most Greek men of his time, he believed women had the same intellectual capacities as men, and his wife and daughter were also philosophers.

EUREKA!

Archimedes is known for his inventions—and his words. Along with pulleys, Archimedes used levers to lift or move heavy objects. Archimedes reportedly once said that he could move the entire Earth with levers and pulleys, as long as he had a place to stand. When solving another scientific problem, Archimedes shouted "Eureka!"—Greek for "I have found it!" People still sometimes use that word when they make great discoveries or solve difficult problems.

FAMILY LIFE AND CHILDREN

In ancient Greece, family ties were strong. Up to three **generations** might share a home, though in later periods in ancient Greece, sons usually started their own households after they married. If one member of a family got into trouble, it brought shame and punishment to others in the family. The children and grandchildren of criminals lost their political rights just as the criminals themselves did.

A father and his close relatives formed the heart of Greek families. The father ruled the household, and laws protected his right to control the others. A mother's main duty was raising the children. When a father died, his property was divided among his sons.

Children

Having children was a woman's main function. Childbirth, however, could be dangerous. Doctors did not have drugs to prevent illnesses or surgical tools to aid in difficult births. Many women died while giving birth, and for about every four children born, fewer than three reached adulthood.

Ancient historians recorded that sickly or unwanted infants were sometimes **exposed**— left in the wilderness to die. Modern historians disagree over how often this happened. An exposed child might be found by a kindly stranger and adopted. Greek men without children of their own often adopted sons. Fathers prized sons more than daughters, so they would have someone to whom they could leave their wealth.

◀ An ancient Roman marble copy of a Greek bronze sculpture of the goddess Hestia *(HEHS tee uh)*. Hestia was the goddess of the hearth and, as such, symbolized family life.

Marriage

In ancient Greece, parents usually arranged their children's marriages. Most girls married in their midteens, but their husbands were often twice their age. In Sparta, however, the bride and groom were usually closer in age. Girls left their homes to live with their new husband's family. A girl's family gave her husband a gift of money or property called a *dowry*. The husband controlled the dowry but had to give it back if he and his wife divorced. In a divorce, children usually remained in their father's household. They also usually stayed there if their father died and their mother remarried.

A GREEK WEDDING

Weddings were festive events in Athens and other parts of ancient Greece. They were held at night and featured a feast at the home of the bride's father. Then the bride rode in a chariot to her husband's home, as depicted in this vase painting. Torches lit the road, and guests carried gifts. The next day, friends of the bride came to visit her in her new home, sometimes bringing more gifts. Spartans, however, did not have such a formal wedding ceremony, and a wedding was not announced in public until the wife became pregnant. A Spartan bride lived with her parents until her husband returned from his long-term military duty, when he reached age 30.

SHELTER AND CLOTHING

Remains in Olynthus *(oh LIHN thuhs)* in northern Greece, the Asia Minor town of Priene *(pry EE nee)*, and other archaeological sites offer some clues about Greek housing. Most homes were built of dried mud bricks placed on a base of stones. Because the weather was usually warm, people did many things outside, and houses tended to be small. The home of a rich person often had more rooms than that of a poor person. This was especially true outside of a city, where there was more land available.

▼ A **terra cotta** model of a Greek house, or possibly a temple, from the 700's B.C. Later Greek houses almost always had a dining room for men. Some also had shops where the owners made or sold goods.

Inside the Home

In most Greek homes, the rooms surrounded a courtyard, where residents took fresh air and did many of their chores. Larger homes had separate kitchens and bathrooms. Spartan homes, in general, were smaller and simpler than ones in Athens or other **city-states**.

The inside walls of many Greek homes were covered with plaster, and roofs were made of clay tiles. A hole in the roof served as a chimney for the cooking fire. Simple houses had dirt floors; more elaborate houses had at least some rooms with stone floors. Water usually came from a well or a cistern—a large stone tank, sealed with plaster, in which rainwater collected.

The Greeks often wore beautiful jewelry made of gold, silver, and other metals. Gold became more common after Alexander the Great sent back gold he captured in Persia. Thin strands of metal were often twisted together to create designs for pins, earrings, and rings. Gold was also used to make bracelets, such as these featuring the heads of wild beasts. Both men and women used a fibula *(FIHB yuh luh)*, a pin used to fasten a chiton. The pin was often decorated with tiny images of people or animals. People were often buried with their favorite jewelry.

Clothing

Greece's generally warm climate meant people did not need layers of clothing. In their daily lives, most Greeks wore a simple garment called a **chiton** *(KY tuhn)*. This clothing was usually made of wool or linen. A chiton had no sleeves and was worn with a belt. Its two sides were fastened at the shoulder with a pin. A woman's chiton reached her ankles, a man's reached his knees. Some Greeks wore another garment over their chitons. Called a himation *(hih MAT ee on)*, this lightweight cloak was draped over the left shoulder and wound under the right arm. In cold weather, the Greeks wrapped themselves in a cloak called a chlamys *(KLAY mihs or KLAM ihs)*. At home, most Greeks went barefoot. Outside, they wore sandals; men at times also wore boots. Both men and women wore various kinds of hats and caps. In Sparta, **helots** were forced to wear animal skins, so they were easy to tell apart from citizens and other residents.

FOOD

From figs to fish and beans to barley, the Greeks ate a variety of foods. The Greeks typically ate three meals a day, and wine was their main drink. Dinner was usually the largest meal, especially for the wealthy. Breakfast was often simply bread soaked in wine. The most important daily foods came from grains—mostly wheat and barley. These grains were made into breads, cakes, and a soupy dish called porridge. The Greeks also ate plenty of fruits and vegetables. Onions, garlic, cabbage, lettuce, and cucumbers were common vegetables. Fruits included figs, grapes, apples, and pomegranates. Honey was used to sweeten foods, and such spices as dill, oregano, and mint added extra flavor.

Food for Body Strength

The Greeks ate such protein-rich foods as fish and fowl. Eel was a popular seafood among the wealthy. The Greeks also ate cheese made of goat's or sheep's milk. The Spartans ate a simple stew made with beans. Wealthy farmers ate meat from cattle, sheep, and other livestock they raised. Meat also came from hunting such wild animals as deer, wild boar,

▲ A **relief** sculpture from the 500's B.C. shows a scene from a banquet. A symposium *(sihm POH zee uhm)* was a banquet for men at which the guests ate and drank while lying on couches, then discussed art and **philosophy.**

pigeons, and ducks. For most city residents or poor farmers, meat was only available at the sacrifices held during festivals. One popular prepared food was sausage, in which grains and vegetables were mixed with meat and fat and stuffed into cow, hog, or sheep intestines.

Food for Athletes

When they trained, many Greek athletes ate special diets. They tried to eat as much meat as possible and avoid bread. Athletes often came from the wealthier families, so they could afford to eat meat, which was expensive in some parts of Greece.

ATHENA'S OLIVES

Olives were an important part of the diet in ancient Greece. They were usually turned into oil, and diners dipped bread in it or mixed it with other foods. Some olives were eaten whole. The olive tree had a special place in Greek mythology. In one story, Athena and Poseidon competed to be the patron deity of the then-unnamed **city-state** that would become Athens. Poseidon gave the city a spring, which symbolized water and trade, but the water was salty and the citizens were unable to drink from it. Athena gave the people an olive tree, symbolizing food, oil, and wood. The citizens dedicated their city to Athena, naming it after her. According to legend, the tree given by Athena grew near the site of the Acropolis, and all other olive trees were said to come from that one. The olive trees near Athens were said to be holy to Athena, and olive oil from them was the top prize for athletes at games held in her honor.

◀ A Greek **terra cotta** statuette from the 200's B.C. of a woman preparing food. Some Greek houses had two or more rooms set aside for storing and preparing food. Cooking was done over open fires inside the kitchen.

EDUCATION

Most Greek **city-states** did not have public schools, and very few children received a formal education. Most learned what they needed to know from their parents and other relatives. Educated slaves might also teach their masters' children at home. The wealthy could afford to send their children to private teachers. Most girls, however, did not take classes, though a few learned how to read, and Pythagoras taught women at his school. Some teachers, called sophists *(SOF ihstz)*, traveled from city to city teaching such topics as grammar and public speaking.

Schools

Greek education changed over time. In the early days of the city-states, boys would memorize and recite poems, especially those by Homer. Later, in Athens, separate schools existed to teach younger boys a variety of subjects. One school focused on reading, writing, and mathematics. Other schools taught music and physical education. One important goal of education was to produce citizens who maintained good **ethics** and followed traditions.

When they were older, sons from wealthy families went to schools run by well-known **philosophers**. Plato started the Academy, and Aristotle ran the Lyceum *(ly SEE uhm)*, where his students lived

▼ *The School of Athens* (1510-1511) by the Italian artist Raphael *(RA fih uhl)*. The fresco in the papal apartments in the Vatican in Rome includes most of the great teachers of ancient Greece, though they lived at different times and did not teach together. In the center, with the white beard and red robe, is Plato. On his left is Aristotle.

A **terra cotta** statuette from about 500 B.C. of a writer at work. The Greeks adapted their alphabet from the Phoenicians during the 700's B.C. In later centuries, most writing was done on papyrus *(puh PY ruhs)*. Strips were cut from the papyrus plant, laid side by side, wetted, and allowed to dry. The dry strips formed a kind of paper.

while taking classes. At these and similar schools, students studied law, medicine, or **philosophy**. Young men also received military training so they could help defend their city-state.

Spartan Education

Sparta had special training for its young. The boys strengthened their bodies through athletics and learned how to fight. Many learned how to read and write, and they also learned songs about religion and recited lines from Homer's *Iliad*.

Unlike the other city-states, Sparta paid for its girls to attend school. The leaders wanted to make sure women were prepared to become mothers. In school, Spartan girls danced to help strengthen their bodies, and they sang songs about Spartan history.

ARISTOTLE ON EDUCATION

In his book *Politics*, Aristotle wrote: "Education should be one and the same for all...it should be public, and not private —not as at present, when everyone looks after his own children separately, and gives them separate instruction of the sort which he thinks best; the training in things which are of common interest should be the same for all...Further, it is clear that children should be instructed in...reading and writing—not only for their usefulness, but also because many other sorts of knowledge are acquired through them."

Sports and Games

To the Greeks, developing the body was as important as developing the mind. Physical education was first tied to military training, to produce fit, skilled soldiers. Later, meeting to exercise or swim became a social activity, and athletic events were an important part of religious festivals. The Greeks prized men who showed their strength or skill in sports.

Places for Athletes

Greek boys and men trained and played at a *gymnasium* (*jihm NAY zee um*), a word still used today. The word *gymnasium* means to *exercise naked*. The athletes practiced and competed naked, so they could freely move their bodies. A gymnasium had an outdoor space where men ran races, threw spears called javelins, and threw the discus. A gymnasium also had a room set aside for wrestling, and the Greeks boxed as well. Some gymnasia also offered classes in **philosophy** or other subjects.

The most important spot for Greek athletes was the **sanctuary** at Olympia. There, every four years the **city-states** honored Zeus during the Olympics. During the month of the festival, the Greeks stopped their wars so they could send their best athletes to compete. The first Olympics took place in 776 B.C. and had only one event—a foot race. Later events included wrestling, boxing, and throwing the javelin or discus. Horse and chariot racing were important events at the Olympics and the other Panhellenic Games. One Olympic event even featured runners in armor. Winners received olive wreaths.

◀ A Roman marble copy of the *Discus Thrower*, originally created by the Greek sculptor Myron between 460 and 450 B.C. Throwing the discus was an ancient Greek sport and remains an event in the modern Olympics.

The athletes did not compete to get rich, they simply wanted to honor Zeus and show their skill. Their home cities, however, might reward them with parades or prizes. Only men competed in the major festival games. In Sparta, however, women took part in athletics, and a race for women was later added at the Olympics.

Other Games

While the Olympics were only for individuals, the Greeks did play some team sports. One used curved sticks and a ball, like modern field hockey. Another was similar to rugby or soccer. Children also had less physical games. These included rolling wooden hoops and playing knucklebones, which was like jacks.

▼ A Greek drinking cup decorated with a painting of men competing in a foot race. The most important running event at the ancient Olympics was a sprint of about 210 yards (192 meters). This race, called the stade *(stayd)*, was also part of another event called the pentathlon *(pehn TATH lon)*. In the pentathlon, athletes showed their skills in five different sports, which also included throwing a javelin and a discus, jumping, and wrestling.

A STAR ATHLETE

Milo of Kroton *(KROH tuhn)* was one of the greatest athletes of the ancient Olympics. In 540 B.C., he won the wrestling event held for young boys. As an adult, he won the wrestling competition five times in a row. According to legend, Milo liked to exhibit his strength by daring others to move his fingers when he held his hand out. No one ever could. According to legend, he once carried a bull around the stadium at Olympia, killed it, then ate all the meat—in one day.

DECLINE AND FALL OF ANCIENT GREECE

A new era in Greek history began with the rise of Alexander the Great. From his base in Macedonia, he conquered the areas of Greece to the south and then set off to fight the Persian Empire. By 326 B.C., his combined Greek and Macedonian forces had reached as far east into Asia as India.

The Hellenistic Age

The period historians call the Hellenistic Age began with Alexander's death in 323 B.C. Greek rule and **culture** spread from its base along the Mediterranean Sea across large parts of Central Asia. The Greek language was spoken throughout the **empire**, and Greek building styles appeared as far away as Afghanistan. At the same time,

Greeks living in foreign lands learned local ways. In Egypt and other lands, some Greeks worshipped local gods.

Alexander's death led to several decades of war, as his generals battled each other for power. Eventually, three separate Greek kingdoms and several smaller states emerged out of Alexander's empire. Macedonia and Greece were ruled by a family called the Antigonids (*an TIHG uh nihdz*). Several Greek **city-states** joined one of

▼ The empire of Alexander the Great touched three continents: Europe, Africa, and Asia. Greeks ruled parts of Central Asia, including what is now Afghanistan, for hundreds of years after Alexander's death.

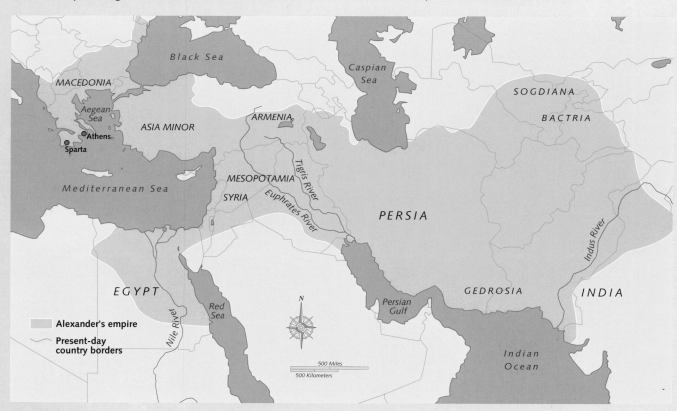

Alexander's empire

Present-day country borders

A mosaic *(moh ZAY ihk)*, or artwork made up of small tiles, found at the ancient Roman town of Pompeii shows Alexander the Great leading his army at the Battle of Issus, in Syria. Alexander's forces defeated a Persian army led by King Darius III.

two leagues, to work together against Macedonian control. Most of the Greek city-states, however, were never truly independent again.

The Rise of the Romans

The Greeks were a major presence in southern Italy for centuries. But by the 200's B.C., the Italian city of Rome had become a major power in the western Mediterranean. In the 140's B.C., Rome extended its control over Macedonia and Greece. In the decades that followed, the Romans also conquered all or parts of the Greek kingdoms left from Alexander's empire in Asia. In 30 B.C., Egypt became the last of the Hellenistic kingdoms to fall under Roman rule.

The Romans adopted many Greek ways. They studied Greek science and associated their own gods with those of the Greeks. For example, Zeus was tied to the supreme Roman god, Jupiter. Roman artists copied Greek styles of architecture, painting, and sculpture. Greeks living under Roman rule continued to win fame as writers and thinkers. Together, the Greeks and Romans created what is sometimes called Greco-Roman *(GREE koh ROH muhn)* culture.

ALEXANDER THE GREAT

Alexander the Great believed he was related to some of the great heroes of Greece's past, and he wanted to rule all of Asia. As a boy, Alexander studied with Aristotle, and during his conquests, he brought scholars and scientists with him. But Alexander is best known as a brave, skillful general. Wounded in battle eight times, he was always ready to fight another day. Alexander wanted to march even farther across Asia, but his homesick troops refused to keep going. His successes led to a lasting Greek influence in parts of Asia.

LEGACY AND PEOPLE TODAY

In A.D. 395, the Roman Empire split into eastern and western halves. The western Roman Empire crumbled in 476, but the eastern half remained and was called the Byzantine *(BIHZ uhn teen)* Empire. The Greek-speaking Byzantines carried on the Greco-Roman **culture** in the eastern Mediterranean region for another 1,000 years.

The Rise of Islam

Starting in the 600's, the Byzantine Empire sometimes battled Arabs who followed the Islamic religion. These Muslims conquered parts of the old **empires** of Alexander the Great and the Romans. In the 700's, Muslim scholars began to translate Greco-Roman works into Arabic. The ideas of Plato, Aristotle, and others influenced new generations of students.

During the 1000's, Christians in Spain began taking back lands in their country under Muslim rule. European scholars soon discovered the works of Greek and Roman thinkers that had been translated into Arabic. The scholars then began translating the works into Latin, the common language of Christian Europe. By the 1200's, Europeans could read many of the great ancient Greco-Roman writings.

▲ A performance of Sophocles' *Oedipus Rex* in traditional Greek theatrical style in London in the 1990's. First performed in Athens in the 420's B.C., the story of King Oedipus *(EHD uh puhs)* of Thebes still fascinates theater audiences today with its timeless themes of human ambition, jealousy, and guilt.

The Renaissance

The rediscovery of these works helped shape the Renaissance *(REHN uh sons)*, an artistic and intellectual movement that began in Italy during the 1300's. Renaissance **philosophers** stressed the importance of the individual and the use of reason, just as Greek philosophers had. European artists began to copy Greek and Roman styles, and scholars taught Greek literature. The Renaissance drew on Greco-Roman ideas and helped shape European thought on politics, art, and education. Even into the 1900's, many American and British students were taught classical Greek and Roman works in their original languages.

Modern Greece

Today, Greece is a modern nation of some 11 million people. Many of the old **city-states** are now just ruins, but Athens is the nation's capital. Tourism is a major industry in Greece. Many people come to see ancient sites where the Greeks developed **democracy**, literature, and other important elements of Western culture.

▼ The U.S. Supreme Court Building in Washington, D.C., is modeled after ancient Greek buildings. The design suggests the ties between Athenian and American ideas about democracy and justice. One statue on the building shows Solon, a lawgiver from ancient Athens.

ATHENS TODAY

Athens, the greatest of the ancient city-states, is now a mix of old and new. The remains of the Parthenon and other buildings dot the Acropolis, while in recent years the city has built a new highway, airport, and railway. Much of the new construction came before the 2004 Summer Olympics. The first modern Games were held in Athens in 1896, and the 2004 Olympics honored Athens's role in both the ancient and modern Games. In 2004, one field event, the shot put, was held at the site of the original games at Olympia.

GLOSSARY

agora An open area in the center of a city lined by shops and public buildings where people met to talk about politics and other events.

altar A platform on which a sacrifice is offered, usually by burning.

archaeologist A scientist who studies the remains of past human cultures.

artifact An object or the remains of an object, such as a tool, made by people in the past.

artisan A person skilled in some industry or trade.

boule A **legislative** or advisory council in ancient Greece.

chiton A simple wool or linen garment worn by both men and women in ancient Greece.

city-state An independent state consisting of a city and the territories depending on it.

civilization The way of life in a society that features complex economic, governmental, and social systems.

comedy An amusing play or show having a happy ending.

constitution The fundamental principles according to which a nation, state, or group is governed.

culture A society's arts, beliefs, customs, institutions, inventions, language, technology, and values.

democracy A government that is run by the people who live under it.

empire A group of nations or states under one ruler or government.

epic A long poem that tells of the adventures of one or more great heroes.

ethics The study of standards of right and wrong.

expose To put out without shelter; abandon.

generation The members of a family born around the same time.

helot A member of a class of slaves or serfs in ancient Sparta.

hoplite A heavily armed foot soldier of ancient Greece.

judicial Relating to courts and justice.

jury A group of citizens selected to hear testimony and give judgment on a legal dispute.

kouros A statue of a naked teen or young man walking with his arms by his side.

legislative Having to do with making laws.

metic A resident foreigner in an ancient Greek city who had some of the privileges of citizenship.

myth A sacred story.

mythology A body of sacred stories about such topics as gods and the creation of the world.

nutrient A nourishing substance, especially as an element or ingredient of a foodstuff.

oligarchy A form of government in which a few wealthy people have the ruling power.

oracle A shrine where people came to seek advice, or the prophets or prophetesses who gave that advice.

order Any one of several styles of columns and architecture, having differences in proportion and decoration.

ornate Highly decorated.

peninsula A piece of land almost surrounded by water, or extending far out into the water.

phalanx A formation of heavily armed foot soldiers, such as **hoplites.**

philosopher A lover of wisdom; person who studies **philosophy**.

philosophy The study of human nature and such ideas as the meaning of life and the best way to live.

relief A sculpture in which the figures or designs project from their background.

ritual A solemn or important act or ceremony, often religious in nature.

sanctuary A sacred place.

stoa A covered walk or porch, used as a promenade or meeting place in ancient Greece.

temple A building used for the service or worship of a god or gods.

terra cotta A type of baked clay used in many different ways. Terra cotta is often used in fine art—for example, vases, statues and statuettes, and decorations on buildings are sometimes made from terra cotta. It can also be used as a construction material.

tragedy A serious play having an unhappy ending.

tyrant An absolute ruler in ancient Greece who took office illegally.

ADDITIONAL RESOURCES

Books

Alexander the Great: World Conqueror
by Michael Burgan (Compass Point Books, 2007)

Ancient Greece
by Peter Chrisp (DK Publishing, 2006)

Ancient Greece
by Anne Pearson (DK Publishing, 2007)

Ancient Greece: Archaeology Unlocks the Secrets of Greece's Past
by Marni McGee (National Geographic, 2007)

The Ancient Greeks
by Virginia Schomp (Benchmark Books, 2008)

Ancient Olympics
by Jackie Gaff (Heinemann Library, 2004)

Empire of Ancient Greece
by Jean Kinney Williams (Facts on File, 2005)

Greek Myths
by Rob Shone (Rosen Publishing, 2006)

The Life and Times of Socrates
by Susan Zannos (Mitchell Lane Publishers, 2005)

Web Sites

http://www.ancientgreece.co.uk/menu.html

http://www.civilization.ca/civil/greece/gr0000e.html

http://www.metmuseum.org/toah/ht/04/eusb/ht04eusb.htm

http://www.museum.upenn.edu/Greek_World/Index.html

http://www.perseus.tufts.edu/hopper/text.jsp?doc=Perseus:text:1999.04.0009

http://www.perseus.tufts.edu/Olympics

http://www.theoi.com

INDEX

Acknowledgments

The Art Archive: 1, 35 (Museo Nazionale Taranto/Gianni Dagli Orti), 6, 26, 30, 40 (Gianni Dagli Orti), 7 (Olympia Museum Greece/Gianni Dagli Orti), 8 (Heraklion Museum/Gianni Dagli Orti), 13, 16 (Museo Archeologico Nazionale Naples/Gianni Dagli Orti), 14 (Archaeological Museum Sparta/Gianni Dagli Orti), 17, 29, 38, 48 (National Archaeological Museum Athens/Gianni Dagli Orti), 21, 49 (Kanellopoulos Museum Athens/Gianni Dagli Orti), 22, 39, 53 (Musée du Louvre Paris/Gianni Dagli Orti), 27 (Agora Museum Athens/Gianni Dagli Orti), 32 (Neil Setchfield), 43 (Museo Nazionale Palazzo Altemps Rome/Gianni Dagli Orti), 45 (Museo Capitolino Rome/Alfredo Dagli Orti), 47 (Archaeological Museum Florence/Gianni Dagli Orti), 50 (Archaeological Museum Istanbul/Gianni Dagli Orti), 51 (Siritide Museum Policoro/Gianni Dagli Orti), 52 (Vatican Museum Rome), 54 (Museo Nazionale Terme Rome/Gianni Dagli Orti), 55 (Museo di Villa Giulia Rome/Gianni Dagli Orti), 57 (Museo Archeologico Nazionale Naples/Alfredo Dagli Orti); **Bridgeman Art Library:** 15, 23 (British Museum, London), 20 (Museo Nazionale Taranto), 33 (Museo Archeologico Nazionale Naples), 46 (Pinacoteca Capitolina, Palazzo Conservatori, Rome/Alinari); **Corbis:** 9 (Chris Hellier), 11 (Jonathan Blair), 31 (The Gallery Collection), 41 (Wolfgang Rattay/Reuters), 42 (Francis G. Mayer), 58 (Robbie Jack); **Getty Images:** 44 (Mansell/Time Life Pictures); **Shutterstock:** 5 (Vangelis), 59 (Gary Blakeley); **Topfoto:** 25 (Alinari); **Werner Forman Archive:** 12, 19 (British Museum, London), 24 (McAlpine Collection), 28 (Ariadne Gallery, New York), 34.

Cover image: **Shutterstock** (Vangelis)
Back cover image: **Shutterstock** (Joop Snijder, Jr.)

Quotations:
Page 17: Camp, John, and Elizabeth Fisher. *The World of the Ancient Greeks*. New York: Thames and Hudson, 2002, p. 85.
Page 42: Freeman, Charles. *The Greek Achievement: The Foundation of the Western World*. New York: Penguin Books, 1999, p. 267.
Page 53: Aristotle. *Politics*. Translated by Benjamin Jowett. The Internet Classics Archive: http://classics.mit.edu/Aristotle/politics.8.eight.html